INFUSED WITH THE MUSE

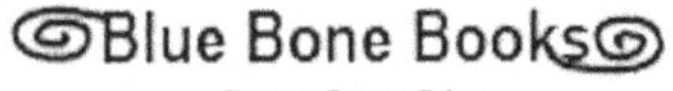

Santa Cruz, CA

Other Writings by
Barbara Thomas

Living with the Spirits of the Land
Celebrating the Magic of Jim's Road
The Burned Woman
Healing Burned Woman (DVD)
Council of Gnomes (Blog)

INFUSED WITH THE MUSE

POETRY, PROSE & RAMBLING THOUGHTS

Barbara Thomas

Infused with the Muse: Poetry, Prose & Rambling Thoughts

Interior design by Melody Culver
Cover design by Robin Lysne
both designs in conjunction
with
Barbara Thomas

ISBN-13: 978-1-948675-08-6
Library of Congress Number: 2021913054

Published by Blue Bone Books, Santa Cruz, CA

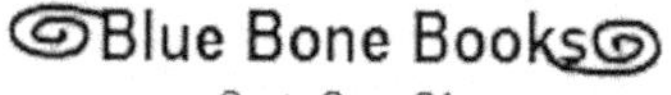

The Muse

When life comes to a pause
and I don't know where to go
the Muse steps in
to get the show on the road

A line for a poem floats through my head
If I jot it down quick and get out of bed
She will continue her story a line at a time
revealing suggestions for action in this life of mine

Contents

GRIEVING & DEATH

MOTHER EARTH

TEA SPIRIT

My Service

is to awaken consciousness

To the spiritual dimension of life

Interacting with the Angelic and Elemental

World of Nature.

Preface

Nearly all the poems and writing I have put into this sharing have come from my journal or were created in writing group.

.db.

There are notes I make for myself that I have kept in this manuscript to share my personal process.

The .db. registers for me an inner code established for inner guidance. The .db. records when I have a deep involuntary breath, which is a signal from the Holy Spirit that I have just named a truth.

+ / -

I do not edit my writing as it comes, I just let it flow. If I were to stop in the middle of writing, it would shift me out of a flow of inspiration and into my mental, thinking mind.

If I have a question about accuracy when I have completed writing, I use my pendulum for yes and no answers. The **+** means yes and the **-** is no.

You'll see this in "Dithering Without Direction."

The Real Barbara Thomas

On August 19,2020, ten days after I turned 93,
my sweet cottage burned to the ground
in the Santa Cruz fires of 2020.
I evacuated to live in my apartment in Capitola Village.

With the help of my son Peter, I started plans
to rebuild immediately.
The words, "I am going to build a Japanese-style house"
floated out of my mouth without ever touching my mind.

My Guiding Spirits were immediately present
to support me through this trauma and transition.
Their first guidance was to tell me that
the burning of the cottage was a "sacrificial offering."
Now, eight months later, a hint of the story has been revealed.

The night that Jim died, early in 2004,
when I went to bed, an audible, loud, sarcastic voice said,
"Will the REAL Barbara Thomas please step forward?"
I was shocked. The voice was so strong and powerful.
I was intrigued; I had never lived alone.

I wondered, just who is the Real Barbara Thomas?
I was challenged, curious and excited
to find out just who IS the Real Barbara Thomas.
I was ready for the adventure of self-discovery.

Jim and I had planned to live in Europe that summer,
starting with a tour of Ireland with Mara Freeman
and ending the summer with a workshop and tour of Wales
with our teacher, R. J. Stewart.

I decided to invite a friend to go with me on the Irish tour,
to come home between trips,
then take another friend to the workshop and tour of Wales.

Both of the trips were focused on visiting
Neolithic monuments and ancient sacred sites.
I met a part of myself in the cairn at Loughcrew
and had another transformative experience in Wales.
I returned to Europe for the next two years
to visit sacred sites in Cornwall, Scotland, and England.

Opportunity came to study tarot with Pamela Eakins,
which I did for the next seven years.
Now I use the tarot as a daily conversation and for guidance
with my Council.
For more than four years I studied the Umbanda teachings
of the elements and elementals with Tina de Sousa.
In all of these travels and studies, I was picking up parts
of the Real Barbara Thomas.

From 2014 through 2020, I spent time every day
for the three months of summer
doing small ink drawings, using a stick from the land,
recording the energies of the spirits who live in the sacred site
on my own land, the Amphitheater.

Last night it was revealed that the transition is in process.
The sweet little cottage I shared with Jim
in the heart of the redwood forest
was the home of Barbara and Jim Thomas.

The new Japanese-style home I am building
is the residence of the Real Barbara Thomas.
The musings in this book record the years of transition.

WAKE UP

It Is Time to Wake Up .db.

It is time to wake up
from our stupor and sleep

The angels
and Ascended Ones who guide

Little by little
a piece here, a piece there

The angels piece together
a very large picture

Revealing who we truly are
and why we are here

Invitation to Wake Up

February 2014, age 87

WAKE UP
To a new dimension of living
To the consciousness of the Seventh Golden Age

MOVE OUT of the matrix of collective consciousness
Out of the shopping mall mentality
Out of the fear of being different
Out of concern to speak your truth

HERE AND THERE PEOPLE ARE WAKING UP
Waking up to the truth of their inner being .db.

WAKING UP TO THE REALITY
They are more than they know
More than their mind
More than their body
More than their family, their history
It is their soul that makes them whole

WAKE UP TO THE REALITY
We are more than humans who have a soul
We are souls having a human experience

THERE IS MORE TO US THAN WE REALIZE
We are not alone
We have an inner life, an inner reality
We are a part of a very large picture
We are a part of a very large consciousness
A consciousness that is love.

LOVE EXPANDS AND CONNECTS
Fear contracts and separates

LOVE EXPANDS AND CONNECTS US
With a large matrix of spiritual beings
With angels, Ascended Ones, Masters and elementals
With those who make up the Company of Heaven

WAKE UP
To the assistance, the intervention
The help that is available
We are not alone
Some set intentions to connect with this reality
Others offer prayers

OUR JOB
Is to act on our inner guidance
To take responsibility and ask for help
To name what we want
For ourselves, our family, our world

OUR JOB
Is to live from the inside out
To be honest, open and free,
To let people see who we really are
This takes the rawest kind of courage

IT IS OUR JOB
To be courageous, to be original, unique, different
To be who we truly are

THIS IS OUR GIFT TO LIFE
Our gift to the evolution of the human race
Our gift to the earth
Our gift to God

Women Wanted

The Call goes out: Women Wanted
To be true to yourself, to live in your power

Women wanted to save the world
Women wanted to serve the world

Women wanted to be strong for their sons
And teach them to be strong in themselves
Strong in truth.
Strong in virtue, strong in humor
Strong in kindness, strong in God.

Women wanted to guide their daughters
To honor their bodies, their minds and hearts
To feel good about themselves
To see their own needs are met
To teach them the good life, laugh and play with others
To create beauty, be kind and support those in need
To stand in their power and fulfill their own dreams

Women wanted to love their husbands
and teach them how to love .db.
To accept their weakness and call forth their strength
To open their minds and hearts by sharing
her own truth and vision of a life fulfilled together

Women wanted to share the truth of their knowing
To demonstrate another way of seeing life
To see life from the heart's embrace
To release mind's fix on knowing best and being right

Women wanted to open to the world of Spirit
To align with Father/Mother God
To bring the mind and heart of God into harmony
In their own lives

Women wanted to live a life of prayer and intention
To call on the angels to guide and protect loved ones
To pray for the end of all conflict whether in the
neighborhood, the schoolroom or the battlefield
To pray for honesty in government
To pray for politicians to become statesmen
With the highest good of all in their mind and heart.

Women wanted to pray for the protection of innocence
Little boys, little girls, elders,
Puppies and cattle, chickens and pigs

Women wanted to embody the presence of Divine Mother
To hold vision for the highest good of all
To know their own value in the world
To know and live within the power of
Being women

Awaken and Become

For thousands of years
my soul path has been to
Awaken and Become

To Awaken and Become
more and more of my true self
lifetime after lifetime

The goal is for my Soul
to Awaken and Become
totally, completely
who I really am

Lifetime after lifetime
to Awaken and Become
more and more of my true self
my God Self

Now I am 86 years old
On December 22, 2012 we entered
the Seventh Golden Age
The times are upon me
to awaken from the amnesia of the false self
to awaken to the possibility of the true self
the Soul

Awaken and Become
to be willing, to be willing
to give up the false sense of self
that is so familiar, so comfortable

where there is
no need to do anything
but float downstream
with everyone else

This is my life to remember and return
to Awaken and Become
This is my life to swim upstream
like the salmon
to swim upstream to the place I was born
to release this life's seeds
and die

Die to the old
Die to the human
to Awaken and Become
to fulfill the seeds of my new life
Dying to the old
awakening to the new
the possibilities

And slowly, inch by inch
choice by choice
to Become who I truly am
to Become my true self
to Be my true self
to Awaken and Become

The question is:
Will the Real Barbara Thomas
Please step forward?

Rise and Shine

I did not come to the planet to hide
I came to the planet to wake up and shine

That my light may be seen
That my light may awaken those who still sleep

That we all might remember who we are
That we all might remember why we came

May we recognize and own our special gifts
May we recognize and own our call to serve

Most important, may we have the courage to do it.

May we have the courage to fulfill the promises
We made to God
When we asked permission
To come to the planet during this time of change

We did not come to the planet to hide
We came to the planet to wake up and shine

WHO I AM BECOMING

The Adventures of a Creative Life After 80: Prophesy & Guidance

When I was 77 years old, I had an amazing thing happen that changed my life the evening Jim died. I returned to my bed, I heard a loud inner voice with a challenging tone say, *Will the Real Barbara Thomas please step forward?* I realized I had never lived alone, and decided to explore just who the real Barbara Thomas was, and is. Now at age 93, I think I have made it.

At age 79, while visiting a Faerie Glen in Ireland, this thought came to me: *When you turn 80 you will start the second book of your life; not a new chapter, but a totally new book.*

At my 80th birthday celebration, my Umbanda teacher said, "*Tiempo* is not for you, Barbara. You are just beginning your work."

An astrology reading for my 80th birthday focused on the writing I would be doing. At that time I was not a writer, other than in my personal journal and participating in a writing group. The astrologer said, "With the planets aligned as they are, there is no way you can avoid writing."

When I turned 80, I broke my leg and was in bed for seven months. During that time, I became concerned that new people were moving onto the mountain road I lived on and cutting wonderful old trees. I thought, *They don't know what they are doing. They don't know this land and its magical history.* Realizing I was the only one alive who knew the original founders and their history, I decided to record what I knew, and to interview the children of original residents and friends.

At age 81, I self-published the DVD *Healing Burned Woman*, a companion to the book, *The Burned Woman*, which I self-published at age 70. I was inspired to use the book as the basis for a workshop to assist healing women to move into their power, and needed to create a DVD of the paintings in the book for presentation in the workshop. For the narration, I had seen a documentary narrated by an English friend and I loved her beautiful voice. When asked if she would narrate my DVD, she told me she had cancer and we should record the narration soon. And so the DVD was created.

At age 86, my gnome companion and teacher, Mano, asked me to write a blog sharing my experiences with him and his teachings. When I did not act on his suggestion, he suggested I ask my friend Mary Jane De Piero if she would write his blog. She accepted, and so our collaboration began. We published a blog on the first of each month for five years, until she died.

In 2014 at age 87, I self-published the book, *Celebrating the Magic of Jim's Road,* which was begun during the time of the broken leg.

At age 91, I self-published my biography, *Living with the Spirits of the Land*, compiled and edited by Mary Jane de Piero.

At age 92, I picked up writing the blog and soon will reach my 100th offering.

At age 93, just days after my birthday, my sweet home named Amity Cottage in the Santa Cruz Mountains burned to the ground. While sheltering from COVID and creating plans for my new home, I gathered all of my rambling thoughts, poetry and prose together in this book, *Infused with the Muse*.

When I first heard that the cottage my husband Jim and I had lived in had burned to the ground, an inner voice said, *This is a sacrificial offering*. My son Peter asked, "What are you going to do, Mom?" Words came out of my mouth without ever touching my mind, "I am going to build a Japanese-style house." I love the floor plan of my new timber frame house, which has a similar size and footprint to the cottage but with a high ceiling in the main room.

I call this home Amity Lodge, the home of the Real Barbara Thomas.

The Muse

I do not think of myself as a poet
I simply am lucky enough
To recognize when the Muse wants to speak

And close enough to paper and pen or computer
To record what she has to say

When the Muse Arrives

When the muse arrives
she must be attended to immediately.
She is not willing to wait
for a quick phone call or email.

Unfortunately, that is my morning learning,
my morning lesson.
I was excited to write what she said
to share with my writing group today.

Now she is gone.
Phone call made, email written,
and now no Muse,
no remembering what she had to say.

Oh well! Oh hell!
another lesson, another learning.

Oh yes! Oh, she is giving in.
I am beginning to remember.
Not as clearly as before,
just an inkling of memory.
I will see if she will swing by again
to inspire me.

Guiding Spirits

I have two guides who live in my inner world
One for 25 years, the other for 30
They are my sacred cord
from my human to my divine

One is an angel connecting me
with the Heavenly Father
The other is a gnome
connecting me to Mother Earth

I have two parts of self
one is a nun, the other a gypsy
The nun is proper, obeys the rules
aligns with the love of the Divine in a life of worship
The gypsy wears bright clothes, big earrings,
loves drama, loves life, celebrates the Divine in all things

The Woman on the Mountain combines them both

The gypsy speaks to the Nun .db.
Take time to live
Give yourself space for beauty
Your body is on the earth
Bring spirit into the body, into life,
to celebrate the Mother's beauty
rather than false teaching to negate,
denying life for spirit

The nun would hide as a hermit
allowing Mother Church to take care of her needs
The gypsy would celebrate and bring Spirit into life,
dress with elegant simplicity
use magic to meet her needs
The Woman on the Mountain is honest, open and free
to let people see who she really is
both nun and gypsy

The nun would be a martyr
would do without, be thrifty, deny her needs and desires
The gypsy would live her truth
celebrate her abundance, live life to the full

The Woman on the Mountain
lives in elegant simplicity
in a quaint cottage in the forest

When the Angels of Inspiration Knock

When the Angels of Inspiration knock
I need to open the door and walk in
to the words and ideas that are present

When the Angels of Inspiration knock
if I wait for a more convenient time
the door sticks. It won't open
The angels of inspiration are no longer present

Their present, their gift
is only alive in the moment that it is offered
Their present—their presence—
is only available in present time

When the Angels of Inspiration come
I am given one thought to intrigue me
I can quit with that one thought as a treasure to ponder
or I can let one thought lead to the next
and a larger picture is revealed

When the Angels of Inspiration knock
and I take the first step through the door
I am led on a winding path
with many possibilities and many plans

When my writing teacher asked
What journey will you take this summer?
the Angels of Inspiration knocked
with the idea to take a two-month Summer Journey
a vision quest to discover my soul path

My Summer Journey was a daily trip out my front door
to get into Betsy, my off-road vehicle,
and drive to the Amphitheater
to spend hours in nature.

The result? My soul path is as it always has been
even though I didn't know it
Now at 87 it is clear:
I serve Mother Earth. I serve all of her children
the angels and elementals of earth, air, fire, and water

The Angels of Inspiration instructed me:
First, complete your book
Celebrating the Magic of Jim's Road
There you will see yourself from a different perspective
You will see yourself
as the Angels of the Mountain see you

When that is clear, and you know
the Divine Plan for your life
Write the next book
Living with the Spirits of the Land
the magic of living a dedicated life

Now I wait, and when the Angels of Inspiration knock
I will walk through that door and follow their lead

Step by step, one step at a time
until the next adventure is complete.
This book in your hand
was their latest call

Intentions

The way I look at intentions
is to become a partner with God

Two ways of looking at living an intentional life:

PHYSICAL
What you think about comes about
What you feel you make real

SPIRITUAL
God has given his angels charge over thee
to guide thee in all thy ways

Angels pick up your intention
and create a pattern of consciousness
Then give it to the elementals to fill it
with substance and form

Betwixt and Between

Today is writing class
I am supposed to bring something to share
I don't know what to take
I don't want to write
I don't know what to say

As I move into my third Saturn return at age 90
I feel I am doing cartwheels through daily life
Everything is changing
Nothing is settled

I don't know whether I am right side up
Or upside down
I get the picture of hanging on a rope
Trying to swing from one side of a canyon to the other

I am betwixt and between
What can I say? Nothing is solid
Everything is different

This has happened before
I know it will pass
And come together in the future AT LAST

I am hoping at Winter Solstice
When the light starts to return
I will see where I AM

I know I will be guided, the next step revealed
I am on my way home
The way will be shown

ps. "On my way home" does not mean to die soon; it means the energies of the future, the Seventh Golden Age, are at work.

Dithering Without Direction

October 2011, age 84

I am in the studio, dithering without direction.
Once again pondering, *Who am I? What is my life about?*

Things I have already established:
I am an artist, which for me means painting.
I have barely kept my artist alive for the past eight years
since Jim's death.

In that time, I have traveled to Europe four times
to visit sacred sites in Cornwall, Glastonbury, Ireland,
Wales and Scotland.
I completed my DVD, *Healing Burned Woman*.
It is full of my paintings, the work of my Artist.
If I had not painted, I would not have had illustrations
for the story I had to tell.

I am fuzzy on this, perhaps
avoiding what I know to be true.
It is hard to form the words.
Is this residue from the Burning Times? +

I easily say Divine Feminine
It is hard, today, to say Mother Earth.

Yet in my deep heart I know:
As an Angel + of the Great Mother +
the Divine Feminine + Akasha +
I am on the earth to assist the planet?+
Mother Earth, to make her shift in consciousness? +
Humanity, to make its shift in consciousness?+

Art is my healing mode, my way of transforming energies +
My way as Magician to bring in the Sacred Fire
in color and form? +
to create patterns of healing energies for the nature spirits to pick up and use? +
for the angels to pick up and use? –

The angels inspire me, direct color, shape and relationship;
the Elementals take them for use. +

I am suddenly aware of a Master Gnome sitting in front of me. .db.

The Work you are doing is OUR WORK
to guide your knowing, acting and living.

Thank you for coming. I didn't realize these meandering thoughts were going to end up, once again, unraveling who I AM and what I am about. .db.

It makes sense when I remember the angels Akasha saw with me: a mother angel, Sho Shona and an earth angel, Era Lyn.

Back to being the artist. My little drawings, which Rama the angel tells me are my most important work, are Transformative Drawings for situations, recently for Mother Earth and earlier energies of place and people.

I have not done those little drawings for six weeks at least.
I didn't have a little pad and didn't go to buy one.
This week I bought two and then found I had one empty
and one almost empty,
so I have been ignoring my calling. .db.

THE MASTER GNOME SPEAKS

It is not time, it is ATTITUDE, not even consciousness for your mind and heart to know this truth. We will not go into what to do about that today.
I simply need to state the truth and put your attention on it. Then you can change, make a new choice.

We have brought you bits and pieces of information for many, many years, even before you came to the Mountain, for your Master Gnome Mano has been watching over you, grooming you to see if you will wake up to your calling and the promise made on entering the earth. .db. The wake-up has come through art.

You are an intuitive artist.
We would like you to act as a trained artist who knows her art has to be seen, shared, explained.
For you have had specialized training
in a specialized type of work.

You are exceptional, exemplary in every way.
Stand up and be counted.
You have been trained by Nature,
through your feelings and intuition.
We have shown you paintings and artists with styles
we want you to incorporate in the Work
you are doing for Mother Nature.

Am I painting FOR Mother Nature or is Mother Nature painting through me?

You are painting FOR HER, under the guidance
of the Master Gnomes, who know exactly
what she needs to see, feel and absorb.

It goes into the atmosphere and is viewed by the elementals; the energy is taken out and spread around where needed.

We would like you to paint small enough so your painting can be taken around and shared. Find a briefcase and cut black paper to size, mask the frame and go to work.

My paintings are for the healing of the planet, Mother Earth. The energies of the colors are guided by a group of earth angels and the form by elemental beings, who then distribute the etheric energies where they are needed.

I, Mano, will speak now.

We have been through this many times in the past, Barbara, and now it comes to this day when we do not want to have to go back to square one ever again.

Today was not actually back to square one, but is material we thought was clear within you. Sit in the violet flame to remove the dross. What has happened in the past, we have given you clear information and you understood, yet the old patter of not knowing, not believing is not cleared and you come back to be reassured again and again. "Is this really true, is that really me?" Well, my dear, let me be the first to say it is NOT the "me" in you. It is the I AM, and this is what we want you to move into—a new way of being, a new form to work within.

You can continue to maintain your humility and the low key that you are comfortable in, when there is no need to show up. And when it is time to show up,

WE WANT YOU THERE
IN ALL OF YOUR GRACE AND BEAUTY. THE ARTIST.

This is to take clear form when you introduce your DVD to friends or groups. We have created a wonderful product, professional in every way. Stand up and be proud, proud of us who have guided you, opened and closed doors.

You are not your own. You were bought with a price of our time, love, patience and guidance, gifting you with teachers, the Amphitheater, your studio, and everything you have needed, Gretchen, Marigold, Keven, Daren, all professionals of great skill. Each have loved your work and enjoyed working with you.

That is all for now. Print this out and read it every day, to make your commitments and set your attitude.

All in love, under the direction of Mother Earth, our planet, our home, the one we owe our lives to.

At the Edge of the Void

Painting the moon, age 84

The edge of the void
is enticing
inviting
distracting

It would be easy
to get lost
at the edge of the void

Never
to enter the mystery
Never
to return HOME

Promises

I can almost remember
the day I asked permission to return to the planet
once again

I can almost remember promising God
This time I will remember the promise I make
every time I return

Once again, dear God, I promise to be happy
Once again, I promise to be healthy
I promise to be creative
and Oh, dear God, I promise to live in abundance
and to share my abundance with others

My heart fills with comfort as I hear God say
Yes, my daughter,
and now I make my vow and promise to you

I will send guardian angels to watch over you
to guide you in all of your ways
You will never be alone
My love will always be with you

I promise that
you will be happy
you will be healthy
you will be filled with creative ideas and ability
and, Dear One, you will live in abundance
and I ask that you share your abundance with others.

I Am Grateful

March 2016, age 89

I must hold my heart steady
as my home and land shifts round me
I must focus my mind on
what I want to happen
and control the ruminating thoughts
that would review over and over
what I don't want to happen

I call for the angels to see
that I always have a responsible
caretaker present on the land
to care for me

I call for angelic solution to the question
How does spring water get to the Guest Cottage?
I call for solution to the leaky roof
over the bed in Forest House and in Amity Kitchen

I give thanks that my needs are always cared for
I give thanks for a quiet focused mind
I give thanks for inspiration and intuition
I give thanks to all the guides that guide
I give thanks for the honor of living in the forest
I give thanks that I am capable
to solve all of the needs that arise
I give thanks and I am grateful
to be alive

I am grateful that I am not
living in the comfort and care of a retirement home
Thank you, God

Soul-Infused Personality

My Soul came to the planet in 1927
with the purpose of
being a forerunner of the Seventh Golden Age.

I consciously entered the spiritual path in 1960.
When attending a Christian retreat,
I received the gift of the baptism of the Holy Spirit.
This baptism meant one thing
to the Christians praying for me.

My soul had another focused intention.
She told me that She, as the Holy Spirit, would be my teacher
and not to connect again with the current Christian
Holy Spirit movement.

She opened the door to meet and trust the new church janitor,
who asked if there were any prayer groups.
The answer was *no*, but there is one woman
interested in prayer: Barbara Thomas.

When I met Gene, an elder with bright, shiny eyes,
we were immediate friends.
Each week we met as he cleaned the Sunday School rooms.
We had prayer and talk of the metaphysical world.

Each week he would bring me metaphysical books,
the big blue ones like Blavatsky and Steiner.
One day I complained,
Gene, I don't understand a thing I am reading.
He responded, *That's all right, Barbara,*
keep reading. Your soul understands.

A soul vision was given in 1975,
Attending a Sunday talk by Torkom Saraydarian.
He said we were all to become soul-infused personalities.
That was it. I knew that was true for me.
I prayed regularly to become a soul-infused personality.

And now, 45 years later, my soul brought
a young man to the Mountain to live
and to work for me on a weekly basis.

We sat outside, he to my right.
When I turned to speak with the person on my left
I felt an Orb of Love filling the space to my right.
Revelation unfolded in meditations that followed:
This young man is part of my soul family.

My soul brought him to live and work with me
as a soul gift to open my heart to soul love,
and in that process become a soul-infused personality.

Revelations began to unfold.
I was told: *Your service is to reveal*
the spiritual dimension of life by interacting with
the angelic and elemental world of Nature.

With this revelation,
I gave myself permission to speak.
My soul became free for deeper work within me.

Working with angels and elementals
is an important part of the emerging consciousness
of the Seventh Golden Age.

Homecoming

Stepping out of the ashes and that which was
Stepping out of the ashes to be guided from above

Stepping out of the ashes
To a new form of love

Stepping out of the ashes
To a new life yet unknown

Releasing my own thoughts
For the consciousness of God

Coming back to the beginning
When first I left my heavenly home

ANGELS

Angel Waiting Room

There is a place in the spirit world
called the Angel Waiting Room
It is a place where angels gather
sitting side by side, telling stories, making jokes
to pass their time away

They are the Angelic Guardians
assigned to people on earth
They have patiently waited
from the time of their human's birth
Wow, a call comes in on the angelic amplifier
Each angel gets excited, hoping it is their person

One gets up proudly to answer their person's call
The others sit back, still waiting
each praying under their breath
I wish my person would call me

Angels

Angels have nothing to do with formal religion.
Angels have everything to do with evolution,
personal devotion, heart yearning,
evolution of humanity and the earth.

Their job is to guide, guard, and protect humans
so they will live harmonious lives, be happy,
healthy, prosperous and creative.
Psalms names it: "God has given his angels charge
over thee to guide thee in all thy ways."

Because we humans are free-will creator beings,
the angels cannot intervene in our lives
without our permission.
I feel that this new evolutionary opening
of naming what I want and setting intentions
is a way that gives the angels permission
to assist us in achieving the things we want.

There are hundreds of thousands of angels
on assignment to help humanity move
into higher consciousness.
Each person has a guardian angel
assigned just to meet their needs.

Unfortunately, if one does not believe in angels
or relate with their angel, or call on them for assistance,
the angel is helpless; they can only hint and nudge.

And if lack of belief moves into fear
of the nonphysical, non-apparent world,
the angel simply leaves and goes to another dimension
within the heavens to wait,
ever mindful of the light in the heart of their human.
Always aware of what is happening in their life,
always hoping for a call for assistance,
for a relationship filled with love and light.

Angel in the Fire

The coals in the fireplace spoke to me
Yesterday as I looked in the fire
I saw the image of a gnome
who stood in the center of a cavern
He was dark and the cavern filled with red-hot coals

I put a log on the fire and destroyed his home
Immediately I wished I had followed the thought
to take his picture
I wished I had taken the time
to look for the camera

Today when I looked in the fire
I saw an angel with wings outspread
I stopped and did not put a log on the fire
Today I went for my camera
By the time I returned the picture had changed
The angel's wings were not as clear .db.

Today I ask the fire angel, *Are you speaking to me?*
Did the gnome wish to speak?
Did the angel wish to speak ?

Apparently not
There was no answer
At least I asked
At least I was ready

Little Glowing Angel

I may be little
I know I am small
but in my heart
I am very tall

My love for you
is great and grand
and if you let me
I will glow and expand

My gift is joy
delight and fun
full of surprises
to bless everyone

You are my focus
my delight and love
I come to live with you
with blessings from above

The Golden Angel

While I paint, writing what I see inside as I look within.

Looking within
to see the feeling of this past year, at age 88,
the first thing I saw was sticks or stakes
in the ground
one after one, after one, after one.
It felt like being fenced in,
almost a wall of stakes.

As I put the marks on the page
at the bottom, line after line
I felt streamers tied to the top.
Streamers that would blow in the wind
if the wind were blowing, as it is.
They softened the stakes.

Now looking at it with blurry eyes
and from a distance,
they look like pilgrims walking the path
to the Holy One, or are they
following the Holy One up the path?

Filling in the space, I made a wavy line
from left to right with a second line
softening the curve.
This now looks like ocean foam and waves
white on a sweet blue ocean.

Another curvy line above,
like the beginning of a heart,
I colored as close to pink as I could find.
And in the middle of colors on the rough paper
I see the figure of a golden angel leading the pilgrims.
This is the picture of my feelings this year,
what I have experienced.

At first feeling blocked in, fenced in,
as cancer entered the lives of Anne, John,
and once, concern for Donna.
As I walked the path, step by step
I determined to hold steady. .db.

And the sticks creating the fence,
instead of blocking me
became a support for stable walking,
moving forward step by step.
Ever feeling the presence of the golden angel
guiding me, I move on.

Now what was the ocean
has become snowcapped mountains
with a green grassy mountainside.
I wonder if my uncried tears
watered the green and growing land.

The freedom to cry came when my heart was touched
by the love of friends ministering to Anne with song.
The golden angel walks in an orb of pink heart love.
Love is the way. Love is the power.
Love is my call.

GRIEVING & DEATH

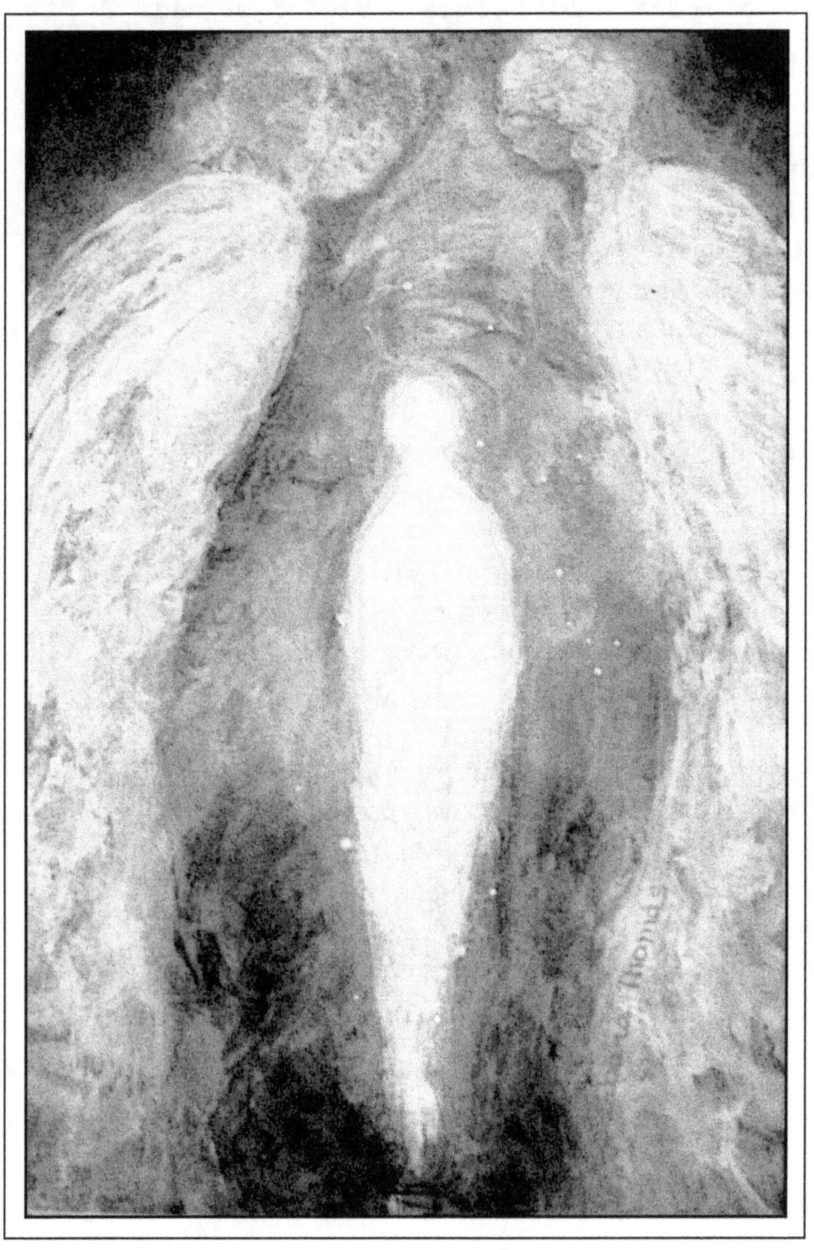

Goodbye Dear Jim

To my dear, dear Jim
And so my dear, it was one year ago today you died.
My year of mourning is complete.

Mourning, m-o-u-r-n-I-n-g and morning, m-o-r-n-I-n-g.
Only the *U* makes the difference between.
That was the year of letting go,
looking back to what was.
A year of, "Last year we were together
and now you are gone."

That way of looking back is full of You – *U* – moUrning.
Mourning your death. Mourning my loss.
Mourning what was and is no longer.

And if the *U* is removed from mourning
as you have been removed from my daily life,
then I am left with morning. Dawn.
New beginnings. Light out of the darkness.

Present time. Now time, future time.
When I look to the past, you are present.
When I look to the future, I AM present.
Each anniversary was a letting go of the past.
You are gone. I AM here.

Each anniversary was a letting go of the past,
of the darkness, of the loss,
and a hello to the present, the dawn, the light.

When I look to the present, to the now,
only I Am here.
I AM all that I have.
I AM that I AM that is present.
I AM me. I AM now.

I AM the dawn.
I AM the light.
I AM moving on with life.

Goodbye my dear.
I AM that I AM that is present
Here and Now.

Grief, Choice & Gratitude

The day that Jim died
I saw a photo in the newspaper
of a very beautiful woman
with a very sad expression on her face

The caption said
her husband was a great movie producer
who died three years ago and
she can't get over his death

I thought
what a loss for that beautiful woman
to grieve so long
I made a pledge to myself
I will not let that happen to me

I learned
to give total respect and attention
When the waves of sorrow came upon me
I would lie down and sob
as long as grief was present

If I stayed in bed, again, and again,
like the waves in the ocean
when the first wave of sobbing subsided
another wave of sorrow would pick me up
and sweep me back out to sea

I realized I was at a choice point
Do I let each wave carry me back out to the sea of grief?
Or do I stand up and step out of the ocean?

I chose to get up
and return to my day's activity
grateful for that which I had once experienced
and was currently grieving

I would then recite my Gratitude Mantra
I am so grateful
I am so grateful
with every breath of my life
and every beat of my heart
I am grateful

Grieving

My mother died
while having dinner in her favorite restaurant
with dad and her favorite childhood friends
wearing her favorite pink suit

I grieved for three years
I was not prepared for her death
I lost my connection with God when Mother died

When Dad died one month after suffering a stroke
ten months after mother died
I had time to prepare for his death

I created a ritual, visualizing my current age and Dad's age
"Dad, please forgive me for any ways I may have hurt you
Dad, I forgive you for any way you may have hurt me"
I did not grieve Dad's death

Year by year, back until my birth
I forgave Dad
and asked him for forgiveness

Death's Gift

Death brings an end
and a beginning.
When a baby is born into this world
it comes after the death of living in the world of spirit.
When death comes
at the end of life in this world
it opens the way to return to the world of spirit.

When Jim's dad died,
my neighbor came to share a quote
from a French philosopher.
"When a baby is born,
the whole world rejoices
and the baby cries.
"When a person dies,
the whole world cries
and the person rejoices."

The night my daughter Anne died,
I woke from a dream hearing her singing,
I am free, I am unlimited
there are no chains can bind me
I am free, I am unlimited
right now....right now.

While I was so sad my beautiful daughter was dead,
the dream and song told me she was alive and rejoicing.

In the Body or Out of the Body, Life Goes On

I had three experiences with my daughter Anne
the last week she was in her body
and the week after she left.

The first was a vision. I had a flash picture of her
sitting in bed totally well, strong and healthy.
My hopes rose.
I felt she would have a miracle healing.

The next experience came in a dream:
I was walking with my mother
down a business street.
It was twilight. The stores were closing.
The streetlights had just turned on.

I heard a woman singing.
It was a strong, beautiful voice.
I knew the song and loved singing it myself.
I am free. I am unlimited.
There are no chains can bind me.
I am free. I am unlimited. Right now.

I had the knowing; Anne was going to leave.
And she did, two days later.
I am told she had a smile on her face as she died.

I now realize the vision of her sitting in bed totally well
was showing me what happened for her
when she left her body.
In a body or out of a body, Anne lives on.

My third experience with Anne came
the week after her death.
I was looking at my life and relationships
with friends and family,
looking at my strengths,
feeling sad at my weaknesses.
What I wanted to change.
    I heard Anne speak into my thoughts,
    I can help you with that, Mom.

It Feels So Good to Cry

Tears
are such a good friend

They allow the body
to release the sadness
the pain

and express
the love that is within

The Good Death

In the beginning our ancestors
walked and talked with the angels.
The door between worlds was open.

That which was will be again.
The soul returns to earth over and over
to practice dying.

Dying is one goal of birth
to create a beautiful death
a conscious death
a love-filled death.

The death goal is to open the door
between physical and nonphysical worlds
between earth and heaven.

The purpose of the good death
is to abolish the idea of "the end"
and open the door of continuous living
the door of new beginnings.

In a body or out of a body, I Live.

The Only Time to Live & Love Is Right Now

When I realized my cottage had burned to the ground
with nothing left of 93 years of gathering, saving
and family memories,
with nothing left of the many binders
filled with past writings,
binders filled with my proposed next book.
Nothing left. Nothing left
of my wardrobe,
my jewelry, my gemstone collection.
Nothing left, nothing left.

My angelic council moved in immediately
to guide my thinking,
to guide my way of being,
to keep me grounded and steady as I start
to rebuild my life.

The first thing they said:
The burning of your cottage
was a sacrificial offering.
They did not say exactly what that meant.
Things I wonder about: Ten or more
houses on upper Alba Road burned.
Mine was the last to go.
Firefighters were able to hold the line at Jim's Road.
None of my other properties or neighboring properties
on Jim's Road burned.

The angelic council reminded me of a statement
they brought to my awareness years ago
to focus and embody its truth:

What is, is . . .
everything works together for good
for those who love

Their next guidance was to love all that has been lost.
When I think of an object that is now gone,
I am to love it. Spend time with it,
remember where I got it, any memories around it,
heartfully love it . . . and let it go.

I just realized this loving memory and release
of items I have loved
is to honor their place in my life,
to honor the consciousness
I imbued upon them as we lived together.

On some level I do not understand just now,
my love gave them life
beyond the life they had before
they came into my home.

My love gave them life, they were companions.
With my clothes we traveled the world together.
My purple suitcase became home away from home,
the container for all the possessions I needed
as we traveled.

And once again they sang me a song
I learned forty years ago.
The past is gone . . . The future is just a dream
The only time to live and love
Is right now . . . Right now . . .
The only time to live and love is . . . right now.

A Baby Does Not Die So the Toddler Can Be Born

A baby does not leave
so a toddler can come in
It just happens

A toddler does not die
so a teenager can come in
It is the way of LIFE

The teenager does not leave
so the adult can arrive
The body continues to change
all on its own

This is a matter of maturity and choice
of attitude and decision
of responsibility and action
Attitude and opportunity
appear to be a choice for some

The adult does not disappear
so the soul can survive
The soul is the force
that carries the life from beginning to end

The soul has the choice to continue
in heaven or on earth
to go forth within the New Age
or come back for a new birth

Begin Again

Begin again! Begin again, Begin again!
What else is there to do in life
but begin again?

Each day is a *begin again*.
How else could it be,
since last night was an ending?

The sun goes down,
I go to bed and sleep.
And when I wake,
the day and I begin again.

I think it is the *again* that needs to be explored.
Is this again the same *again* as before?
Or is today's *again* something new?

When Jim died
the *begin again* had to be something new.
A new way to live, a new way to explore.
A new way to be open to what life had to offer
as a person and no longer a couple.

Step by step, day by day.
Each day new, each day a begin again.

How can I look at that now
when so much inside of me has been changed?
Not necessarily removed
but definitely different.

How can I explore this invitation to begin again?
I think it is more in the naming: This is a *begin again,*
and then doing the same routine with the consciousness
that this is new, this is different, this is a new beginning.

Or after naming *today,* I shall begin again
and ask, What shall I do today
to support the new beginning?

I'm not sure that is the way.
The challenge is to begin again,
to do the same thing in a new consciousness.
This will take noticing, paying attention.

What is new inside of me, around me,
as I begin again?
Somehow I am thinking the *begin again*
comes at the beginning of each day.

What if I thought of it as going to the studio
to begin again?
That sounds like starting over,
like something went wrong, not completed or satisfactory,
Instead of letting that be the end of it.
Take a deep breath and begin again.

To begin again, there has to be some goal in mind,
some direction I was heading and perhaps got sidetracked.
So I must return and begin again to get back on track.
As I read my Studio Councils with Spirit, I find
many things they have suggested that I did for a short while,
then forgot . . . and never returned.

I wonder at this present in-between place I find myself,
with many things ending. I see no beginning other than to wait
and see what happens.
Perhaps a suggestion or request has been ignored.
If I were to begin again in that direction, I could be guided
to the information and inner experience
that is waiting to reveal the next steps.

I remember many years ago, when I was taught
to work with the Finders (who help find lost items),
I was told to start putting things away
and they could guide me to the lost item.
It is easier for the Finders to guide a moving object
than it is when I simply sit in a chair and say
Help me find my lost item.
Their words were colorful; they told me
to *Stop yammering* and get up and move.

So now I am told to begin again. .db.
I ask to be shown my next step to start moving,
so I can be led and directed to the understanding
which I am waiting to unfold.

A reminder comes . . .
If I say *YES* to life, life will say *YES* to me.

MOTHER EARTH

She Rises

For 300 years
She was scorned
Demeaned, denied
Tortured, burned

Community midwife
Herbalist, healer,
Counselor, friend
The feminine denied
In both women and men

The memory remains
In the collective field
We all share
The tide began turning
December 22, 2012

Now . . .
SHE RISES
again

Returning to earth
Wisdom, counselor
Nurturer, friend
The feminine
in all of us
true to the end

I Remain

I remember in 1985, at age 58
walking the streets
in Glastonbury, England

My heart was touched
when I saw a large plant
emerging through a crack in the cement
I felt her dertermination and will to survive

Today in 2018, I remember
I heard her story
I still hear her singing victoriously

I am here
I remained alive winthin the earth

Even though covered
smothered in cement
Even through no one can see me
I AM still alive

Father-Mother Sun
heard my cries
They sent compassion and comfort
which warmed my heart
and warmed the cement

I was filled with inner power
inner determination to emerge
victoriously

The elements
within the cement
felt my push, my deep desire
They opened their hearts
and let me push through

I greeted the sun
with gratitude and joy
So happy to be free

I embraced the sweet air
as her spirits greeted me
I shouted with joy
to be alive, growing well and free

I was delighted when you saw me
heard my song and the story I tell
Even though you did not Know
your heart heard my song
Singing loudly, I have returned
I cannot be kept down long

I AM the Earth
I AM Mother of all
I sing my song
This is where I belong

The joke is:
If I am not here
if I do not stay .db.
you will not be here either
You can't get away
We are one

Surface Dwellers .db.

Pelour* named *surface dwellers*
as those living on the surface of the earth
I have been a surface dweller
Superficial

I have found what I lost
a sense of worship
a sense of wonder
magic and mystery
a certain respect
an honoring, devotion

Too busy to meditate
and move into the spaciousness of time
Losing the magic of life
of relationship with the divine

Filled with outer life, not enough of the inner
I forgot the Mother's love
her heart of devotion
Whatever I have focused on or accomplished in the outer
is too high a price to pay for losing the love of the Mother

Surface and outer life have dominated
while inner life and depth have suffered
I become shallow, selfish, walking alone
Locked in my head, inside my home
Avoiding fresh air and being outside
This is such a sad story
I discovered and tell

Mother dear, I want to come home
Bridget, please keep the well
I look to thee, I love you

While the truth bears witness
tis the earth beneath me
Pelour named me a surface dweller
but his call comes from the deep

Tis Mother Earth that I love
Tis Mother Earth that loves me
She is real, physical in form
I touch her, walk on her, eat her and more

To light the Sacred Fire
To breathe the fresh air
To walk on the earth
beside the ocean, right there

Bridget, dear Bridget
Goddess of the Mother
keeper of the heart flame
protector of children
All love your name
All things of the earth share your blessings
and are named

To my Council of Gnomes
my teachers and guides
I forgot who I AM
Forgot to step outside
My call to serve the earth
Mano dear, no wonder you have not been with me
All these months I have walked alone

There has been no need
You have done nothing wrong

Integration with Starlight, Jon, and more
Faerie, my family who live within the earth
within the Mother's care

My call is to come home
to Faerie within

The studio, the amphitheater
the walk on the beach
All within Nature
where you are easy to reach

**The Lord Pelour is a little-known earth god of the stature of the earth goddess Virgo.*

Magical Land

Age 90

I live on magical land
When I moved to the Mountain
I met God's other kingdoms
the angels and elementals too

In the beginning
these three kingdoms
inhabited the earth together
in cooperation and co-creation

The Call is out
The planet is to be purified
protected from the polluting actions
of the lost creator race

Selfishness, greed, hatred and war
are to end
Those who pollute the planet
are to leave

A new dispensation has arrived
Angels and Elementals, cosmic beings
and Universal Love are to redeem and restore
that which has been lost

Homecoming
Return to the beginning
Realignment and recovery
are in hand, in store

Chips

Sitting in the Amphitheater one bright sunny morning
I became aware of a group of little gnomes
about two feet high standing in front of me.

In the distance I saw a spirit woman walking down the hill
She had on a long full colorful skirt
I felt she was connected to the little gnomes
and thought, *She must be their nanny*

I immediately felt a rebuttal
and sharp words from the little ones:
That is not so, we need no nanny.
She is our Maria.

She helps us understand things you do
that make no sense to us.
Our Maria tells us that being human is
quite a complicated matter.
She said that you have more chips than we do
and they are not all going in the same direction

We only have a few chips inside of us
and they work in harmony
because they always go the same direction
One thing we do not understand:
It feels so good to live in alignment
with all of our chips going the same way
Why would you ever choose to do otherwise?

Our Maria tells us God has given you free will
and you have a choice to be in alignment or not
We have no choice and actually we prefer it that way

When I returned to the Amphitheater the next day
I pondered what the little ones had to say
I wondered, if my chips all went in the same direction
would I be open to the flow of God's love and inspiration?

With that thought I became aware of the little ones
once again standing in front of me
I told them I had been thinking about being in alignment

I was beginning to understand the value
of having my chips aligned
Their immediate response: *Then why don't you do it?*

Rhyme for This Time

We work in rhythm and rhyme
Our truth to bring forth in this time

We speak what we know
To reveal and to show

To anchor our truth upon the earth
We bring the Seventh Golden Age to birth

After the first rhyme, I looked within and felt excitement
among the group of little elemental beings.
My feeling was that they were happy this contact
had been restored.
I got the feeling of a hole opening from their dimension,
to and through me, to bring forth their truth in simple rhyme.
I thought of Mother Goose-style nursery rhymes
appropriate for this new time.

Iona .db.

To love a man
To love a child
To love a land
A history
A people

To love a life
To love a heritage
To love your ancestors
When that is all you have

I walk the planet
In my mind and my heart
All land, the earth is my home
Wherever I roam

Each morning I must sit alone
To go within and connect this day
With the day before

Where am I now?
Bombay? Srinagar?
Africa? Australia?

The scenes are the same and different
The people are the same and different

Loving hearts, smiling eyes
Silent introspections
All the same and all different

Wherever I am
To start the day
I must go within
To find myself
To be myself

So I can be true to me
Authentic with the people
I am with on this day

To love a man
To travel with him
Here and there
Near and far

To love a land
To love the earth
To find the beauty of each place
Of each person
All the same yet all different

I do not know my European heritage
I do not know the city, town or country
My ancestors lived within

I am fourth-generation American
My dad was from Germany
Germans married Germans
Spoke German, went to German-speaking church

Slowly while in America
The German hold loosened
Dad married Mom
Of French and English heritage

I do not know what town
What part of France
What part of England
My ancestors lived
And now live buried within the earth

I have no sense of loyalty
To Germany, England, or France
The land my ancestors left behind
To move to the New World for a new life

I do have deep love for the Land of Scotland
The barren land of Mull
Hours of driving to get to the ferry
To take me across to the island of Iona

I love that land called Iona
The last time I visited, I felt would be my last
I went out to say goodbye
As the stars left the sky
And dawn began to bring the light

I sat on the ground by the stone church
Using it as a break from the wild wind and cold
I sat on the ground by the stone church and cried

I have been so blessed
To visit you so often
Dear Iona, my love,
Somehow a deep part of my life

I have been so blessed
To spend time with you in spring
When the lambs were just babies
Jumping and playing tag

I have been here in winter
When the storms
Were so wild and windy
It was not safe for the ferry to move

I have been here in the autumn
When the young boys
Left home to return to school
And family and friends waved white cloths
From windows, sending blessings on their way

I have been here on Taty Picking Day
When all the children had the day off from school
To go with their parents and harvest potatoes
From the field to store for winter meals

I remember when I, once, long long ago
Arrived on this land in a little boat
I was a woman and my skirts got wet
As I walked to shore

I remember once, long ago
I lived in the monastery
I was a man learning to paint the Psalms
In a very large book
The Book of Kells

To love a land
To love a man
To love a child
To love myself
I love you Iona
You live deep in my heart
May I ever be as sturdy and enduring as you

May I ever be as welcoming as you
A sanctuary, a place of refuge
A place of raw, rough beauty
A sturdy land with a sturdy soul
Iona

Iona is a small island a short distance off the coast of Scotland that I love and have visited many times in many seasons. Her land is inviting, her history deep and mysterious.

One winter the Findhorn bus let me off at the ferry to Iona, to pick me up the following Saturday. I went to the little one-room grocery store, only to find both hotels closed that winter. The woman rented me a room with a bath down the hall and no kitchen privileges. For a week, I cooked in the English electric kettle: potatoes, carrots, packaged soup and Ovaltine, and ate apples and bananas.

A sweet experience happened as a couple boys were leaving the island to return to the fall semester of school. Friends and family walked with them to the ferry, and others waved white cloths out their windows, sending prayers and best wishes.

Once I stayed at the Argyle Hotel. Every morning at 9, I heard the sound of cow bells and saw an older woman in black boots walking two LARGE cows to the green pasture to graze for the day, then again at 4 I watched her head them back home.

Years later, I sobbed when I heard that 7 of the 8 high school boys who lived on Iona drowned one night as they returned from a party on the mainland. Their boat was capsized by a freak wave rushing up the channel. This brought an end to many years of generation after generation inheriting the land and continuing to live on Iona.

TEA SPIRIT

Mother Tea Speaks to Me

When first I started drinking tea
Tea Mother began speaking to me
a line at a time and often in rhyme
a surprise and total delight to me

There is a desire
From all those who love tea

That there be no distraction
Between thee and tea

No computer focus
Nor iPod disruptions

Only the warmth of cup
Held in both hands

That warms my heart
And opens my mind

To receive inspiration
Of a very unique kind

A thought, a poem, a rhyme
Something different comes every time

I open my heart
I silence my mind

As I sip my tea
The Mother comes to be with me

I am grateful

A Tea Spirit Dwells

Deep in the heart of China
an ancient tea forest grows
One hundred feet tall
one thousand years old

Year after year
generation after generation
tea leaves are harvested
carefully, mindfully, lovingly
by the tea farmer and his wife
Some tea farmers' children
work with tea all of their lives

Tea Spirit Mother

Tea Spirit Mother
stays in the forest with her trees

Tea Spirit Sisters travel with the tea
sent into the world by air and over sea

When visiting a home
Tea Sisters sleep deep in the tea

to be awakened when hot water
pours over the leaves

With joy and delight they do their work
blessing the sippers as they start their days

Holy Sweet Mother

Mother Tea
you nurture me
care for me
enlighten me
with your wisdom
warmth and power
held within the veins
hour after hour

Infusion

When I infuse the hot water
With the leaves of the Tree

Tea Mother, in turn, infuses me
I feel her presence of love, personified

At the end of each tea session
I am totally satisfied
Sometimes even glorified

Thank you, Mother
Amen

Remembering

The Mother
that is tea
the Mother Tree
that is tea
remembers me
and once again
mothers and blesses me

Each time
I sit quietly
heartfully
sipping tea
just she and me

I remember
lives and places
living deep in the forest
long gone and yet remembered

Each time I drink a cup of tea
sipping in quiet
heart-filled spaces and places
I remember

While Sipping Tea

The continuity
of sipping tea, one life to the next
threads a cord of love
with unremembered
remembering

There is a deep secret
with the sipping of tea
heartfully, artfully
blessing you and me

Such a sweet presence
I wait for you
one cup, two,
and many more
maybe five or six
definitely more than four

The pot is small
the cup is small too
each sip is hot
for me and you

God is God
Tea is Tea
the God in Tea
blesses the God in me

There is a magic
in drinking tea
heartfully
soulfully
just tea and me

While sitting and drinking my tea
dear Tanya
I stop to think of thee
and wonder if this morning
you are drinking tea with me

Honoring

Each morning as I sit and drink my tea
my heart opens and thoughts
of the great Ancient Mother
come and embrace me

Thousands of years old
thousands of years
feeding and healing her people

I honor her presence
I think of her trees
growing wild by the rivers
with her leaves blowing in the breeze

MAY MY LIFE BE A FLAME

May My Life Be a Flame

May my life be a flame
to honor all life

May my life be a flame
to bring light to the world

May my life be a flame
to shine forth the Great Mother

May my life be a flame that sends
sparks to light the flame in others

May my life be a flame to bring comfort
to my children as they face the challenges
of life and death

May my life be a flame
that lights the way in the dark

May my life be a flame to expand my vision
and see the larger picture

May my life be a flame that brings the rainbow
of colors into all I do

May my life be a flame that brings
colors alive with life in the
paintings I paint

May my life be a flame
that guides my family to find their own light

May my life be a flame
For my children to be a light for others

May my life be a flame to warm the heart
of the earth with my love

May my life be a flame
as I walk the Divine Plan prepared for me

May my life be a flame to open the way
to explore what the light reveals

May my life be a flame to reveal truth
to my ancestors who lived in the dark

May my life be a flame
of joy to all I relate with

May my life be a flame to warm my heart
to rest within the love of the Mother

May my heart be a flame
alive with the Great Mother's love

May my heart be a flame
of all that has been and all that is to come

May my heart be a flame
that brings comfort to my dear ones

May my heart be a flame that sings joy
with my granddaughter about to give birth

May my heart be a flame
to my grandchildren about to get married

May my mind be a flame that shines
the truth that gives my life meaning

May my mind be a flame
for the Christ of God to bring clarity and justice

May my mind be a flame that reveals
the unknown with clarity and comfort

May my mind be a flame
of truth, respect, and wonder

May my joy be a flame that reveals
the small pleasures that bring great promise

May my life be a flame that enfolds
the light, the love
and the law of the four directions .db.

May my life be a flame of transformation,
transmutation and transfiguration

May my life be a flame that anchors
the future into the present

May my life be a flame
that sees and lives the perfection of the future

May my life be a flame bringing perfection
into the simplicity of my daily life

www.ingramcontent.com/pod-product-compliance
Lightning Source LLC
Chambersburg PA
CBHW050959050726
47592CB00007B/2636

* 9 7 8 1 9 4 8 6 7 5 0 8 6 *